Lift-the-Flap Book

EWW! Critter Litter Southwest

See what critters leave behind!

Stan Tekiela

Adventure Publications
Cambridge, MN

Coyote tracks can look a lot like a dog's tracks.

Coyotes eat other animals to survive. You might find a small pile of fur and bones left over from their dinner. Yuck!

Coyote

If you see a big mound of dirt near a hole in the ground, it could be a coyote den. Coyotes dig a safe, dry home in a hillside for their babies. You might not see signs of a coyote very often. You are more likely to hear them howl at night.

Lift to see what **Critter Litter** the coyote left behind! Eww!

Black Bear

If you find logs and rocks that are turned over, a bear may have been looking for bugs to eat. Bears also love berries. So if you see a raspberry bush picked clean, it might have been a bear having dessert!

Bear tracks are huge. Each foot has five toes and claws.

An itchy back? No problem! Bears rub against trees. It leaves fur and special smells behind. This lets other bears know, "I'm here."

Lift to see what **Critter Litter** the bear left behind! Eww!

Javelinas look like they walk on their tiptoes! The banana-shaped hooves leave unusual tracks.

Javelinas like to eat cactus, especially prickly pear. Ouch! Watch for cactus with big bites missing.

Javelina

The javelina has a thin white band around its neck, kind of like a collar. It looks a lot like a pig, but it's very different. For example, javelinas live in big families, but pigs don't. Javelinas and pigs do have one thing in common: they make a big mess when they eat!

Lift to see what
Critter Litter
the javelina
left behind!
Eww!

Bobcat

Bobcat moms dig their dens under the roots of a fallen tree or in the soft sand of a hillside. If a baby leaves the den, the mom picks it up with her mouth and brings it back. Just like house cats, bobcats scratch up dirt and grass to cover their poop. So be careful where you step!

A bobcat track looks like the track of a house cat, but a bobcat track is bigger.

Bobcats like to scratch trees. Look for long scratch marks close to the ground.

Lift to see what **Critter Litter** the bobcat left behind! Eww!

Mountain goat tracks are wider than deer tracks. This helps it to keep its balance in steep places.

Mountain goats don't wear coats! Their hair gets very thick during winter. In the spring, some of the hair falls out in clumps.

Mountain Goat

Mountain goats have long, curved black horns. The females have shorter horns than the males. Mountain goats usually live in the mountains, so few people ever see their tracks. During winter, mountain goats scrape the ground with their hooves to dig up dead grass to eat.

Lift to see what **Critter Litter** the goat left behind! Eww!

Look for tiny tracks with five toes. The front track is a little longer than the back track.

Ringtails sometimes live in hollow trees. They line the inside with grass and leaves to stay comfy and cozy.

Ringtail

The ringtail is a very unique critter. It has a face like a fox, a body like a cat and a tail like a raccoon. Ringtails can climb trees like a squirrel. They are known for catching mice, voles and lizards to eat. Ringtails are rare to see. They only come out at night.

Lift to see what **Critter Litter** the ringtail left behind! Eww!

Cottontails have very big back feet. Oddly, the front tracks are always behind the back tracks because of how they jump.

Cottontails love plants. If you see some plants chewed off at an angle, they might have been a cottontail's dinner salad!

Desert Cottontail

When resting, a cottontail lies down and flattens its ears on its back. But if it senses danger, it will spring up and hop away very quickly. A mother cottontail makes a nest by digging a shallow pit in the ground. She makes it extra comfy by lining it with soft plants and fur from her chest. She also hides the nest, making it hard for other critters to find.

Lift to see what **Critter Litter** the cottontail left behind! Eww!

Northern Raccoon

Raccoons get food anywhere they can, even from garbage cans! So if your garbage cans are tipped over, a raccoon might have visited your place. To know for sure, look for paw prints.

A raccoon's front tracks look a lot like your hands.

If you find half-eaten berries on a log or a rock, they may have been a raccoon's tasty treat.

Lift to see what
Critter Litter
the raccoon left behind!
Eww!

Mule deer tracks look like hearts. They point which way the deer was going.

Male mule deer antlers fall off in spring. You might find them in the woods or in fields.

Mule Deer

Mule deer have huge ears that look like they belong on a mule! After a mule deer rests, it leaves behind a large oval of flat grass. When it stands, it often goes to the bathroom on that grassy bed. Gross! This smelly spot tells other mule deer, "I've been here."

Lift to see what **Critter Litter** the deer left behind! Eww!

Porcupine

Porcupines climb high in trees to find bark to eat. So trees with missing bark might be a porcupine's dining room! Porcupines also sleep in trees. They only come down when they move to another tree. When they walk, they flatten the grass, so look for their grassy trails.

Porcupines waddle. Their tracks look like a wide, wiggly line from one tree to another.

If you see a lot of chew marks on a tree, a porcupine might have been munching there.

Lift to see what **Critter Litter** the porcupine left behind! Eww!

The tracks are tiny, but look closely. You might be able to see five toes on the back foot and four on the front.

Squirrel food doesn't come in wrappers. It comes in pine cones! Golden-mantled Ground squirrels tear the cones apart to eat.

Golden-mantled Ground Squirrel

Have you ever seen a squirrel with very fat cheeks? Golden-mantled ground squirrels pack their cheek pouches full of food. They take the food to their underground houses to save for later. They need to store a lot of food to last an entire winter!

Lift to see what **Critter Litter** the squirrel left behind! Eww!

Coati tracks are large and wide with five toes on each foot. Wow, those are some long toes!

Female coatis live in a den only while their young are born.